1

FRACTURES

Additional praise for *Fractures*

"Equal parts vision and prophecy . . . devastatingly precise, full of aching desire for a complex past and nostalgia for the future yet to come. Gómez is writing with an urgency for the most pressing issues of our time. This is a voice that demands to be heard."—**Tina Chang, author of *Hybrida***

"Craft and empathy are inseparable; lyrical pleasures resonate with tenderness and sorrow. Gómez's deft control of language—the syntax is nimble, the diction is zoetic—brings us close to the boundless resilience that helps us survive, change. Gómez's work confronts and rebukes, but it also sings."—**Eduardo C. Corral, author of *Slow Lightning***

"Carlos Andrés Gómez is a poet with the courage and skill to look beyond what we think we know and reach toward less comfortable, more nuanced understandings of the turmoil that surrounds us and the turmoil within us. That talent—both honest and humane—shines through these poems. A deeply resonant and moving achievement."—**Matthew Olzmann, author of *Mezzanines***

"Striking, searching, and serious, Carlos Andrés Gómez is a voice I have watched and listened to from afar for years. His poems often leap landscapes beyond the West and ask us to consider the history we have been taught and how we speak it and carry it in our bodies. There is an earned depth and urgency to Gómez as a poet."—**Raymond Antrobus, author of *The Perseverance***

CARLOS ANDRÉS GÓMEZ

FRACTURES

The University of Wisconsin Press

Publication of this book has been made possible, in part, through support from the Brittingham Trust.

The University of Wisconsin Press
728 State Street, Suite 443
Madison, Wisconsin 53706
uwpress.wisc.edu

Gray's Inn House, 127 Clerkenwell Road
London EC1R 5DB, United Kingdom
eurospanbookstore.com

Printed in the United States of America
This book may be available in a digital edition.

Library of Congress Cataloging-in-Publication Data

Names: Gómez, Carlos Andrés, 1981- author.
Title: Fractures / Carlos Andrés Gómez.
Other titles: Wisconsin poetry series.
Description: Madison, Wisconsin : The University of
    Wisconsin Press, [2020] | Series: Wisconsin poetry series
Identifiers: LCCN 2020010786 | ISBN 9780299329945
    (paperback)
Subjects: LCGFT: Poetry.
Classification: LCC PS3607.O4876 F73 2020 | DDC
    811/.6—dc23
LC record available at https://lccn.loc.gov/2020010786

For my mother

Grace & Gabriel: everything
is for you

CONTENTS

ᔕ

HIJITO

for Michael Brown Jr.

I am enthralled by the image
in front of me: my face overlaid
with his—a boy, almost a man, inside
the glass of a grocery store
reaching for a branch
of seedless grapes.

This sly mirror. This taut mirage.
A coiling limb slithers in my gut, its roots
(invisible)—like I am on this asphalt
to any soul that is inside, right now,
like he is. Today, she is
nine weeks along, he is almost eighteen,
and I am grasping for any thought
that is not my son calling out breathless
from the hollow lungs of night, abandoned
seven feet from the hood of a patrol car
where a hubcap swallows secrets
beside a pavement-choked throat
heaving for breath (his jawline borrowed
from my face). Above it, a still-shaking
hand crowned by smoke uniformed
in my skin.

I

POEM ABOUT DEATH
ENDING WITH REINCARNATION

after Matthew Olzmann & Tarfia Faizullah

Blood has its own democracy.
My father & I puncture steaks
& watch them ooze—deep maple
walls eavesdrop as steel teeth

scrape & claw the porcelain
we use to distract our manically
clenching jaws. I'm well practiced
in this ritual: empty & fill, empty

& fill, until there's nothing.
Our filets gone, we sit & stare
at the eggshell table spread,
abdomens swelling like silence—

They found a mass.
She's having surgery next week.
I had always planned for him
to be first. Now the woman

fifteen years his junior, mother
to my twin baby siblings, is dying
or might be. I've been rehearsing
years for this talk, except it isn't—

my father, held only by the dim
lighting that shrouds his silhouette,
reduced to heaving. I envision
the stepmom it took me eleven years

to embrace being lowered carefully
into the damp earth, an old man,
flanked by two teenagers, watching,
& I will be there too: an overcast

Tuesday that no one passing by
will remember, & as usual, I won't
be able to get the dimple right
in my tie. For a second, although

we are nowhere near the mountains,
I will smell the crisp air she so
loved & remember the first time
we walked without the heaviness

of that first encounter both of us
carried for far too long. But on that
unremarkable day for most, a light
rain will interrupt the hike I am on

in my mind, a man will read overly
rehearsed words from a book she
did not believe in, & we will stand
like guards, numb. We will watch over

the sacred earth she spent an entire
lifetime trying to protect, now her
home, flanked by roots cross-stitching
the rich soil, what becomes the promise

kept to those endless rows of buds
ready to push through & that twisted
symmetry just above, a dangled blade
from a mouth chewing in first light.

MURAMBI

Rwanda, 2008

There is no smell of death here. Even the lime
has faded from what it was meant to preserve.
Atop this hill, everything feels small and
possible. I convince myself school is out,
each classroom merely waiting. A holiday perhaps.
The grass, a twisted maze, yields sound
but no music. The battered doors, some still
stained a faint copper, were once tinged with
dark burgundy. When the breeze troubles
their rusty hinges, a pinched song overtakes
the concrete skeleton that remains, rises up
like a warning siren to anyone within earshot.
Midday rests an unrelenting blade against
our faces. A child on the abandoned soccer field
is full-out sprinting as though a stadium
full of souls is cheering him on.
Nothing here will ever again grow. His mother
is somewhere, getting water or gone. The guide,
who will not give me his name or ask for mine,
leads me to what every foreigner thinks
they came this far to see. They still use machetes
to cut the grass: *Among other things*, he reminds me,
it is a most useful instrument.

UNDERGROUND

When my wife boarded the subway
to Manhattan this morning, she smuggled
four centuries beneath the worn overcoat

she inherited from her mother: the coat
her mom clutched on a Greyhound bus
from Tampa to Talladega. The one she

laid across her seat at a rest stop midday
on a sweltering Tuesday in August,
throat parched and palms glazed in sweat,

as she asked for the bathroom key. She
clamped her painted nails as the cashier
refused to offer her a word, instead

pointed to the *White Only* sign and
motioned toward a dung-filled field
where she was forced to squat as

a busload of tourists watched her slide
her drawers to her ankles, trembling
to keep her balance, trying to spare her

church shoes and her grace. There is
a child, four generations from now,
who will remember a story he's never

been told, see himself in a frayed book
about Jim Crow, discover a dung-filled
field behind an overgrown rest stop and

remember a woman he's never met alive
on the wall of his grandmother's foyer:
bloodshot eyes that refuse to look away.

BLACK HAIR

I made a vow
    to join clustered
strands with these
    fingers, careful
as they are clumsy,
    submerged in this
delicate calculus.
    I learn about
love doing this,
    preparing for some-
one who might
    help me understand
all of this better.
    I keep starting
over, as though
    concentration
is where I took
    my misstep, as though
I am not three decades
    behind in my practice.
As though it is just
    a pattern I'm trying
to find (too late).
    I'm too late, I think,
or maybe it's something else: Papi's hands
    never knew how to fix
my sister's hair. I tend to
    each thick, onyx strand
like I'm mending
    her favorite cardigan,

as though my calloused
        hands might coax and
shape anything into an
        ordered grace. I layer
another braid across
        my love's scalp.
I can feel, with each
        pull and twist, the newly
assembled crib watching.

INTERRACIAL IN FLATBUSH, BROOKLYN

Their scattered voices
suffocate the afternoon
lull like sleeping lungs
abruptly filling with
water. We hold hands

flanked by glaring eyes
that refuse to be pulled
free. A man reaches
between his legs, offers
it to my wife, flinging

a mouthful of spit and
epithets toward us.
Each pupil is a dim
swamp flooding, silence
blanketing a shallow body

in Neshoba County, sunset
shedding its absence across
the congealed oven grease
beneath a rusted burner.
A woman's neck swivels

when we pass, wraps
a hard vowel around her
tongue like lighter fluid
choking a glass bottle
holding a fuse. On this

corner, scored by dancehall
and soca, there is nothing
more novel than me and
my love's contrasting hues—
it ignites a rush of color

from these strangers'
faces. They ring us
a violence familiar
as February weather,
mine our skin for

metaphors, demand we
offer answers to questions
forming like infants from
their throats. I have watched
my body's primal wisdom

flicker dark as a fist-
concealed palm, ache
so volatile it screams
mute. Rage is a language
I unlearn at the intersection

of Ocean Avenue and
Church, no shoreline
or cathedrals in
sight, only glass
decorating a fractured

sidewalk. A new
voice pierces the
air, a barrel of pitch
that hits me like a wall
of ice,   bolder

and higher frequencied
than those before, this time
a fiery infant with chestnut
skin and amber eyes,
writhing in a flimsy

stroller, pointing toward
the dimpled oval bootprints
I leave behind in the hazel-
colored slush, squealing:
Papi! Papi!   Papi?

NATIVE TONGUE

I went there to meet a man
with my father's name. We sat,
flanked on all sides by other
awkwardly assembled pairs,
each obsessed with the shapes
of each other's mouths and
the sounds they made. He grabbed
his crotch and slowly unfurled
a word I knew he had
been saving: *espectacular*.
That was the way he described
how he was in bed, taunting
and flirting while shaking his
head disapprovingly at the way
my tongue rolled an *r* like a mouth
anaesthetized by too much tequila,
my mind feeling familiar as the wide-
arched house we lived in when I was
five. I remember beating my open palm
on a screen that was nearly unhinged
by a burglar, or was that just a dream?
Sometimes I search for the exact day
I stopped dreaming in the language
that sings my name. What it felt like
to watch something slowly drift
away without knowing if it might
ever find its way back. I wonder if
I dreamed that night at all. He snapped
his fingers near my face, told me
I needed a lot of work. I'd been doing
this with him twice a week, an escape

from the life I'd built. So I relished
each clumsy syllable like a secret
I was finally being freed from,
trying to learn something from a man
with the same name as the one who
worked so hard to rid me of it.

COOL

Smooth chisel of his calf
against mine, the L.A. dusk
betraying our slow-creeping
city bus, he mentions his *homeboy*
in the Valley, those he just left
in West Hollywood, at church:
the homeboys who have sleepovers
on Thursdays—

Yo, you wanna be homeboys?
Lemme getcha math.

And before I respond, a phone appears
from his hip, face narrowed into focus
like he is readying his mouth to blow
glass. He moistens his lips, steadies
the slight tremor rattling his lower jaw
and then it happens: he unlocks.

I no longer notice the neck tattoos
cross-stitched across his bulging
arteries, biceps the size of small
sandbags, the Kobe high school
throwback that left me in awe
when he got on—only his amber
eyes, now delicate as orchids.

We cool? he prods. *You cool . . . right?*

Yeah. And I'm not sure how to answer
and not answer the same question.
How to carve the top layer
of *cool* without the hot breath,
tune this frequency to the right
key of skin being slapped, how
to hold a damp palm, without hinting
back-to-chest, sweat-laced in embrace,
our skin is touching

                        and I'm trying
to map out the rules of *cool*, his bright
teeth barely holding back a clutter of words
I am trying to outrun, right hip spilling
sideways into my seat. And everyone
on this bus is pretending to be reading
by this point, waiting to see what I will say.

I want to say I have a girlfriend
waiting, that I have no friends
here. I want to say this is the first
compliment this city has offered
me. I want to say I get so lonely
here I might fuck anyone tonight.

It is my stop. Give a nod and turn.
He is waiting for my answer. I do not know
which one of us is trying to escape.

CHANGING MY NAME

Imagine: I could start drinking
cucumber water and change
how I dress. I could eat cottage

cheese on a hemp bagel, buy boat
shoes and evaporate on command.
I could be Andrew Carlos Williams

and wouldn't scare Lindsey's
roommate from the Valley when
I slept over. I'd start overpronouncing

everything and get called back by
apartment brokers. I would raise a son
with a strong Anglo-Saxon name

who'd look even whiter than me
and never get asked where he is from.
He'd decide to drop the accent

mark but his tongue would still catch
on consonants (inherited from his abuelito's
old reading lessons). We'd invent a new

origin story and always stand, mouths
robotic, each hand clutched to chest
in the shape of a colony of flesh.

PRONOUNCED

You excavate anything that has tried to lodge itself
in your body without permission. You bury the toothbrush
between your back molars and scrape whatever

you find. One loss makes you feel all other losses.
Eleven years later, when you no longer eat pizza
or speak Spanish, when your father's profile invades

your clenched jawline, you borrow his brisk gait,
his snort, his face. People say you look white.
Your father never does. The restaurant won't seat

you, the hostess says neither of you meet the dress
code (your father's wearing a double-breasted suit).
You are a man trying to roll your *r*'s again. Where did

the words go? You are still trying to retrieve the sounds
you once dreamed in. You hardly remember your mother
tongue. You are trying to pull something useable from

the wreckage. Yet it all feels familiar. Your best friend
compliments your clean pronunciation, the way you have
learned to let go of everything you once called home.

II

LAST SUNDAYS AT BOOTLEGGERS

My entire wardrobe was Canal
      Street original, knockoff chic,
adolescent sleek in my double XL

blue & black bubble jacket.
      Yeah, I was inside the club
& what? Inside an oversized

coat coated in sweat & Old
      Spice, a kid eyeing sixteen but
not quite there. I wanted it all,

chico: learner's permit,
      the latest Jordans in baby
blue, maybe a wink from

the pretty Boricua from Social
      Studies. & when Biggie's
verse dropped in "Only You"

he was in that room & teaching
      us how to live elevated from
that third-floor wasteland towering

above India Point, so we sang,
      sour throated & nostalgic
for times we hadn't yet lived,

in unison: like we wrote it, till our
          voices cracked & spilled over
& between every rift but in

the throng of lost kids where
          I finally found a self I loved,
it all came together like we

could remix any wreckage
          & make it into a stage
to slay, so we swayed &

grinded like our lives
          were a music video
tribute, hip-to-hip.

KIGALI MEMORIAL

Superman sheets hang in the genocide memorial
identical to the ones I had in middle school—hid
from my first girlfriend as we trafficked kisses,
afraid she might discover I was still a boy.

My thirteen-year-old self confronts this hero,
his rippled body rising, always rising toward
something I could never see, arms outstretched
in endless flight, or was it a kind of surrender?

Eye level with the youth I outgrew,
fingertips pressed against glass, warm
as a father's yawning throat, its unconscious grace.
As the air in my chest thins, I imagine someone

taking my covers and smuggling them to this hill
in East Africa, my adolescence abruptly erased.
What was I so busied with that incessant April?
How many souls perished each time I blinked?

I sift murmurs for the voice of the boy
trapped inside the monument now ensnaring me.
I picture someone inside my ribcage, knitting a scroll
of names. I am fifty-three feet from the Exit,

a small doorway with a low arch that opens
into a lush pasture where 258,000 people
and me, a seventh grader, stretch endlessly
into dust. The sunrays that spill through

the fissure in this room bear light that darkens
the shadows already being cast. The contrast
so stark that parts of the room suddenly disappear
and, for a moment, everything—my childhood

sheets, the strangers' huddled weeping,
photographs of families stacked floor to ceiling,
my restless hands, babies' shoes, an identity
card smeared with blood—is gone.

ELEGY FOR THE LONGEST YEAR

I would wake up just before dawn & try
to escape the teasing light, my defiant body
somehow still above ground & pulsing

while the pavement watched. I never ran
anywhere. I always ended up at the same
place. But I would return, always then, anyway

battered by the sharp wind to a mausoleum
of stacked & scattered cardboard boxes
that rarely had the chance to collect any

dust. Everything I loved was temporary.
It was the morning Tío was killed &
I sat at the top of the stairs of my attic

bedroom. You had twins on the way, Papi,
& I held a calendar that mapped a path
from the sadness & claimed it as my

home. I am a father now counting the days
until my child turns fourteen. My wife calls
it the year that does not end. *We are not waiting*

for anything, she tells me, *not failure or death*
or whatever is to come.
                    Papi, how do I become
half the man you are & not the man you were?

WHEN TWO WORDS FRACTURE THE MIRROR

I

Shoulder and *soldier* were the same
word. My fumbled speech less
that of an immigrant's son, now
able to make something of
the white noise that claimed
everything.

II

My father carried the title of Breadwinner.
Nothing made the clamped jaw of an
afternoon unlatch more quickly and with
as much abandon as when he jogged, much
to my mother's dismay, around our barren
yard in Cyprus while I giggled atop his
shoulders as though gravity had lost its
touch. The war, barely at a standstill,
seemed to hibernate beneath his worn
New Balance running shoes. He made sure
to jog every morning. Ran marathons by
himself: how a man escapes
his finally failing body. How
he transcends the failing image of
what others believe him to be.
The civil war between Turks and Greeks,
made real by minefields that persisted
and the scorched fighter plane whose tail
rose from the dirt near our house,
was not the war. The real war
was home.

III

My grandfather was a soldier
pretending to be someone
he was not: native in German, a Nazi
passport, a dealer of arms. Which
version of us is real? Why did I
obsess about war my entire life,
revel in the flinch of nightfall
scored by explosions, but remain
afraid of guns? Petrified
of that moment a man must face
another man, real or imagined.

THE AFTERNOON YOU MOVED OUT

In our lopsided driveway
that would lure my basketball toward
the busy street, I was shooting
hoops on a seven-foot rim.
You pulled my limp arms
around your waist and told me
the one thing that would make me
stop crying: *I won't make us move
again.* And then gone. I don't

remember the bag you must have
dragged half-open across the lawn
I had forgotten to cut the afternoon
before, or the way my sister must have
sat, turned her radio up as loud as
possible and then watched from
the second-floor window. None of
those memories stick. They are empty

boxes like the cardboard we would
assemble every year or two and use
to hoard more and more bad drawings
and the clothes our cousins had passed
down. I wonder if my daughter will
remember I read to her every single
day I ever spent with her. Or if she
will only remember the times I was

not there: the field hockey game
I might miss in sixth grade, when
prom coincides with a conference
I have no choice but to attend, or
that moment she calls from college
and needs me. I remember the rare
days better than all the others,
cannot recall what you said

before the car door closed, only
the house still haunted
by the endless rolls of half-used
packing tape, the same tape I used
to take lint off the dress shirt Mommy
had picked for class pictures.

C(H)ORD

My voice box is my father in homeroom at thirteen: muted. Minus
    two words: *Thank you*—the only in English he knew. Like

the switch got flipped to Spanish and I am sifting my memory for
    shadows folded into syllables that ghost my throat.

My father's happenstance gratitude and lonely adolescence
    now haunt my larynx. My throat is a Catholic school

hallway crowded with scar tissue and silence. Every thing becomes
    my musicless throat: the labyrinth of concrete above me,

cracked plates stacked on the kitchenette's heaving chest, an unplanned
    window in the hem of my love's plaid skirt, spittle

of ice through the haze of dusk in late December. I try to make
    friends with the silence. Hold its endless weight, tell myself

it is another kind of song. And this, after a life spent filling
    its bottomless silo with noise: each time we moved and

I had no one to call or share my boredom with, I would invite
    invented friends into my bedroom. I would coax them

into my dreams to listen. And they would—sit, quietly, by
    the dresser and let me speak. But now I cannot

do anything but rest my ear against the widening gut
    of that hollow drum of silence, imagine what I will

not be able to hear from my own mouth for another week.
There is no proof I will ever again speak, ever

offer the tuned vibrations of my electric breath to a room
gorged wall-to-wall with the lustrous splendor

of listening. I feast on a banquet of steam, toast with a trio
of trills, yawn my soft palate into grace, start with one

minute of sound then two, four then eight, rebuilding
the locomotive of stubborn flesh that pistons tremors

through my sacred jaw. I am a child's toy learning
to produce a single note. I am sheet music bound to

the shaky hand of a blind man straining his memory for chords
that just minutes ago rose up through his torso

like a flourish of color and foliage in spring. The cord in my throat
that has hemorrhaged from misuse is the same instrument

I must trust with my life to jumpstart my stalled vocal
folds and guide my flawed body back into the world

I have abandoned. Faith is a sanguine apparition I move
my lips toward like a reed I am wetting in preparation

for sound. It begins as a soft rumble that undresses
its pinched frequency, rattles kinetic like a neutron's

frenetic swell of current and then, finally, it's there: full-
bellied thunder, boundless and unbroken.

AT THE PLAYGROUND, ON THE BUS, EVERYWHERE

my daughter is not   flirting

with you   at four months

          she does not yet

know her feet   are hers.

Twenty years   from now   I hope

she knows   her whole body   is hers.

HAND-STITCH

I am holding my friend Gino's hand
and asking the army recruiter for more
information—*About the Marines, please,*
I say. He fidgets with his cuff links,
paws at his first communion crucifix
through his shirt, drags the back
of his hand across the close-shaven
sandpaper of his chin. Gino is staring
him down through the eyeliner he wears
like a middle finger. We watch this stranger:
caught between the trained movements
of a machine and the churned butter
in his body. Just like mine, two months
before when I said *Hell no* to a trip
to the gay club. *I just don't want to lead
anyone on. It'd be like colonizing the space,*
I said. Which sounds a lot better than
*I'm uncomfortable. I wouldn't know
how to stand. What do I do if a song I like
comes on?* In East Africa, I walked
the dirt roads of a township, my pinky finger
intimately wrapped around the smallest
digit of the most infamous guy on the block.
He was my friend. It is how friends
walk the streets there. When I greet
my Iranian friend's father, we embrace
cheeks twice. In Thailand, my host casually
patted my leg at the first family dinner.
I nearly jumped out the window, thinking
he was reaching for something else. Everyone
laughed. A passerby gives me and Gino

matching names. I tongue the word around
in my mouth. Feel the tender sting make
a home in my torso. Stare at the word
Brotherhood splayed across a camouflage
banner. The recruiter stares down
at the table, as though it holds the secret
code to life's great questions. His corrected
stutter and slightly overcompensating
stance blend into the decorations behind
him. So much so that I can barely even
tell he is still there. He pretends we are not.
Begins sorting and re-sorting the three
lonely pamphlets dwarfed by the large
rectangular table where they now sit.
Boys, seriously. I'm just doing my job.
Please—his mouth begs in a voice
so small and human it makes me
feel like I have just blurted out
a secret this man has given his life
to guard   like freedom.

EDGE OF THE DANCE FLOOR

after Terrance Hayes

   What? Are you
a faggot? she asked. My palm
      offered like a fist

   of tulips—*a man takes*
what he wants—as the bassline
      flooded our bodies

   into a starved harmony
of salt. I clawed her waist, the nearest
      corner swallowing

   us whole as her head
tumbled toward a cemetery of three-
      day-old beer. In the epileptic

   surge of strobe, she looked
woman, as all the boys smiled,
      fanged in stage smoke.

   We were told nothing
was off-limits. A shy kid
      in oversized jeans un-

   snapped the bra of the fresh-
man just within reach. None of us survived
      that night. We stand forever

on a precipice
we did not choose, glance back
at the mirages

we became. My eyes
were better closed, fear in the hull
of my gut—all I see now:

a sprawl of men carrying
the ache we recognize better
than the men whose names

we borrow, the grief
umbilical. The night my child was
born, the cord refused

our baby that first heavy gulp
of breath, heartbeat dissipating into
a tapestry of mechanical sounds.

I thought life was the only
question—heavy as an ancient anchor on
my lungs—until my body sighed

as though the gun jammed
next to my temple when I found out
my child was not a boy.

III

ABECEDARIAN FOR THE PIMP I ALMOST TOOK A BULLET FOR

after Natalie Diaz

I

All I knew at twenty-three was the two-sided coin:
bad & good, the world recast in a black & white
cinemascape. I wore a cheap knockoff from 1-2-5th—a
draped-loose bubble coat, my pockets choked with
everything I carried: condoms, brochures, business cards,
fragments of faded receipts (that would shower out with each
grab at my baggy jeans), my wallet & keys. At first, I
had two thoughts walking into the brothel: I need a new job &
I do not want to die. I still taste the punch of cheap incense, still
jump a little when I hear anything steel lock into place.
Kids would play on the mangled sidewalk out front,
leave their toys three stories beneath a chorus of rehearsed
moans scored to an escalating percussion of thumps.
Not once before had I seen a john in the lobby, until that day.
Out of nowhere, an argument swayed the bolted door open,
Papá turned to *Puto*, turned six-eight pimp with the
quickness, turning slurred words into a blur of bloodied
rings & bucked knuckles. *I'm nobody*, I told myself, *I'm a*
social worker, not some Good Samaritan & shit.
That is, until I caught a glimpse of the glinted metal
unveiled midspat from the john's backpack—overtaken by
visceral momentum, I tackled the skinny sap
with all of my weight, hoping my grip would hold.

II

X was a pimp once too. Murdered not too far from here.
You always laughed at the jokes on instinct, while the
zebra-printed miniskirt of a girl crouched low—out of sight.

AFTER THE CAB DRIVER ASKS ME—
HOW YOU LIKE BLACK PUSSY?

And she's on the other side
of the car, a wasteland between
us of worn steel, glass, and blood-
shot eyes that were, at first,

offered me and are now trained
on my right hand's instinctive
clutch, having retracted into
a fist. His glare, which raked

over her silhouette when we first
got in, followed by an admiring
nod my way, as if to say: *You won.*
You got what we're owed. The car

lurches past my slackened knuckles
grazing the door. The sidewalk
emptied of anyone but us: *He gave us*
a free ride? she asks, bewildered—

How kind.

EIGHTEEN IMAGES AROUND THE TEXT MESSAGE TO YOUR MOTHER

silence-choked throat
in unfinished basement

laughter whiskeyed, strewn
father, nightfall descending

layaway furniture, scattered
chest roped   snug

mortgage underwater, rows
of off-white pills,   wife

gone, court order,
smoke syruped to

itch, bloodshot morning
fix, gambler's pipe

bright-eyed giggle,
knuckles, flickered

sun carved open,
a trembling mouth

mother coaxing light
from his shadow

as the screen awakens:
I would like my remains cremated.

THIEVES IN THE TEMPLE

after Jon Sands

On the side of a highway
in rural Indiana
3,246 homemade wooden crosses
stand impassive as deserted
buildings waiting to be gutted.
A sign above them:
Each cross is a baby
a woman chose to kill
today. I consider driving across
the faux cemetery, riding
free and anointed across
its hollowed back, picture
the landscape emptied
as the shops on Main Street.
Flanked by cornfields, I spot
a large church and imagine
its opulent, sturdy pews clutching
a gaggle of worn faces like a fist
of light. I wonder what Jesus
would have done? If the theft
of His good breath would have sent
Him raging toward these brittle
and stiff-jawed men
still scrapping to exchange
their stubborn grief
for a currency tangible
as mistranslated wisdom.
Would He have razed
this pasture, made of it
another kind of house?

A BLESSING FOR THE INTERNET TROLL

When you tell me—*I hope*
you die—and post a meme
of an obsidian-skinned
woman, faceless and stripped,

with watermelons in place
of ass cheeks being pinned
down and sodomized by
a white man in uniform,

and you add a flurry
of laughing emojis above
the looping six seconds
of film, all in response to

a poem, I wonder about
the mother who loses sleep
over your birthday. How many times
have I mistaken pleasure for joy?

I've dreamed about pinning down
my bully in Times Square,
removing a heavy Glock
from my waist and demanding

he strip while tourists livestream
the moment to every person
on Earth. Watch him beg and cry
and suddenly become human.

I block the death threats
these days, delete hate mail
from avatars I know offer a flimsy
veil to what could easily be a scared

boy trying to survive ninth grade.
Or maybe the keyboard hides
a CEO on his off-weekend missing
the daughter who just lost her

second front tooth as he scans
the internet for strangers to troll
as though it is a meaningful substitute
for touch. I wish you a version of

yourself that is better than
mine. A life that ever leaves
you in the wake of its gentle
and endless awe.

REVISIONIST

A year into his second marriage it
appeared: precise amnesia. My father's
inverted symmetry through which

his children are mapped. He cannot
remember to address any of the four
of us by the names he gave. Not

to say he has forgotten them—
instead, my older sister borrows
our younger's name, my younger

brother mine as wrinkles are
ironed out of off-white slacks for
a first date. My father is more

of a father with his second family.
We are more of a family. But I travel
too much like him. He says, *I am*

worried you're away from home
too much, Nico. And, each time,
I am called by the wrong name,

I almost correct him, then wonder
the cost of each small revision and
how it might change that sprawling

unknown in the distance. If I
might someday need his tools
to right my own family again.

INERTIA

The afternoon is turning what's left
of me to sand, and still no rain. My hands

turn into glass. How dare a promise
for something not be kept? Nightfall is off

somewhere holding someone else's hands,
and nothing's left in the streets but rest-

less thumbs and lists to be done. The day stops
rotating on its axis of noise. A single white bird

cuts a silver scar across the sun. And yet,
here I am, a father tasked with suturing

the fractured light. My daughter looks up
at the bird who has, by now, left us far behind.

     Wait, no—This is a spell I am casting.
I told my mom it was the flower shop's fault,

anything but let her know: I forgot her birthday.
I made sure to say I asked for the supervisor, wrote

a strongly worded letter, anything to appear less
small. I cannot help but find a way to change

the story, to somehow remain unblemished.
                  This is what I do.

WHEN OUR BLACK SON ARRIVES

I will go back to my superstitions:
everything in threes, silent prayers,

rubber bands on wrists. A blood moon
will arrive the night before. The road

will lead us toward land flanked
by water on all sides, a formation

of fluttering magpies keeping guard
beneath steel beams. I will convince

myself I am not my father. I will call
my father and ask for advice. His voice

will echo on a three-second delay
as if from another realm. I will make

sure to stop cursing, no excuses,
I will work on my temper, ask

protection from gods I have
never believed in. Our homes will

get bigger but somehow, each day, feel
smaller. I will watch him resent my

jawline and admire my backbone, teach
him to tuck his elbow in on free throws.

I will wait by the door the first time
he takes the car out by himself. I will

have nothing to offer the stoic
night but clasped hands. And then,

I will wait. I will sit beside the front
door and wait.

WHAT HAPPENED

We all know what happened. But
let's say we left the bar four minutes
earlier, by the time it would have
happened we were already in the car.

Let's say we skipped the pair
of birthday shots from the mouthy
bartender. We'd have made
it home, right? Or, let's say I was

seventeen feet closer when
it happened. Say the car
keys somehow found their
way into my hands, I blink,

we're home. Or we
don't make it, I blink again,

we're singed metal across
the median, couldn't make the hard
pull off the Franklin exit. I live. He

doesn't. Or worse: he does. Whatever
is left of him.

We remember the story
we commit to. Then, we tell
ourselves it happened.

Whatever happened: we were celebrating.
All good and well. But let's say, I'd just
broken up with my girlfriend or didn't have
a reason to live.

Let's say I was three inches shorter, or spent
more time measuring the symmetry of
my face, waded through long evenings
with a bottle of Jack Daniels against
my chin pretending it was a pistol.

Later that night, say I'd told the police officer
in the basement of Vanderbilt Medical Center I had
a description. Given a vague account of the guy
and it led to seven random Black men
in East Nashville—on the way to the pharmacy
for cigarettes or diapers or Skittles or
chemotherapy medication—getting locked up.

One gets seven years. A kid loses her father.

Let's say I was standing by Brent's side
when it happened and not across
the street, buzzed and fuming with
my back turned, while he dragged ass
and drunk-called the first pretty
face in his phone.

Say he didn't have eyelashes no one
can look away from, didn't respond
to the guy's girlfriend as she called
out. The fist didn't arrive more quickly
than the moment.

Let's say it wasn't his birthday. We played
another game of one-on-one that afternoon,
one of us sprained our ankle (probably him).
Or I got food poisoning: the lunch buffet
had a bad piece of butter chicken.

I'm not saying I believe in fate or religion.
Or anything. But let's say only one of us
survives.

The guy took another swing, then
another, then used his boot like an ax on the concrete curb.
Or what if a knife came out or a .22.

> He looked like the cartoon of a guy
> trying too hard. A guy no one takes
> seriously, then shows up to work
> in body armor with an AR-15.

> I know what happened, endlessly:

We leave   start to walk up   street and toward

next to the   hotel or maybe it was a building that looked like   and
          I'm
in front of him, or maybe, at first, we were side by side up the

hill. It was early   , and   was out that night.

          It was a few minutes after   o'clock in the
morning, or just before. Definitely close to the hour. I'm sure of that.

          called out first to   .   and they're chest-to-chest

someone   it sounded   like the crack of a
wooden   against

concrete   and he just   like a redwood felled

SUV blocked   EMT smelled like cigarettes   I think maybe
he was smoking?   and he keeps asking the same question

MRI   the same question   fifty-seven staples down his skull

same question   I drive home   seven hours later, hands still

shaking   dried blood

changed the color of my button-down   off-white to dark

burgundy.

the same

question   the   walks   same   in

      the doorway   question

flight   phone call

             his parents   same

      question   the curtains   stayed drawn

                       months.

IV

MEIN KAMPF HAS BETTER REVIEWS THAN ONE HUNDRED YEARS OF SOLITUDE

on Amazon—I found out today,
at the exact moment a sound
like drowning (or heaving) took me
and my ears hostage, as a kerfuffle
of futile scrapping tried desperately
to keep a bird atop a ledge, so as not
to tumble from my fifth-floor air conditioner.

I could tell you: *Nature is breathtaking*
or carefully describe how the scent
of my daughter's sweat-dampened
scalp, just after she's woken and taken
that long drawl of a yawn, is still cradled
by the pillow on my lap where her nape
was resting just sixteen minutes ago, but
what would that prove?

Once, I watched a slight, nervous man
in a starched, pressed uniform empty
a flurry of baton hits on the limp skull
of a homeless man for snatching
a rich woman's purse. Watching, I felt freed
of my innocence, all seven and a half
years of my life seemed to evaporate
into the thick summer air of Central Park.
It was 1989 and I knew, definitively,
for the first time, how easily
I could kill or be killed.

BEFORE THE LAST SHOT

What was I doing at fifteen?
Facedown on the pavement,
nostrils tinged with bullet-smoke,
the brick-dust falling around
us like fresh snow (or white
chalk), his lanky silhouette stalking
the abandoned sidewalk.
It was summer, Brooklyn.
Nothing ever happens
until it happens. That's how my brother-
and sister-in-law were describing
their tours in Iraq after our dinner
in Manhattan. We had decided to take
a shortcut through Sumner projects, then
heard the unmistakable sound that tore
through the story I was telling about
a lunchtime fight on the blacktop of
my high school, a sudden flash
of lightning. No one believed it
was happening. They forgot their Army
training, rubber-necked toward
the source of the thunder. And then we
tumbled behind the parked cars.
Waited. For what, we were not sure.
Between cars, I could only make
out his narrow back and the dark
steel clutched in his small hands.
I needed to see his face, half
expecting to see myself: standing
on that corner aiming at
something that is never quite there.

ABOVE THE SPEED LIMIT

The first time
I got pulled over I turned
to the classical station, rested
shaking hands on the steering
wheel, elevated my voice an octave,
& blinked wide & scared
so he could see the white
of my eyes & emerald irises
in the late May sun. He didn't ask
my name. Never saw license
or registration. Said: *Just take
it easy*. So I did. So I do.
But my son, fifteen years
& three months from his first
driver's test, is Black—what will
he do? How much of my stare &
smart mouth are imprinted? How
will he understand why I can't sleep
each night he's away from home
& I look just like the men
who too easily mistake
the dark silhouette
of his wallet
for a gun?

RACE WAS NOT A FACTOR,

they said. He said, *It*
looked like a demon. It
charged me like I was five, It
Hulk Hogan—

            two legacies
ghost-stenciled into concrete, one shadow
sifted into ash. He sleeps at night—*No*
regrets. His family as certain as the closed lid
of a coffin
they will be safe.

               It happened, he says. *It was*
unfortunate. It is
what it is.

            Which is the invisible
legacy—
            eighteen years of a boy's
stifled blush, choreography
of a scowl with index & middle
salute, sinew flung forward, barrel
chest soft as unmixed concrete, whisker-less
chin line. His crown was bursting
forth & bowed, inverted king
posing for a peon graced with steel, skull
twice knighted by fire. The final blade
of light cut endless through the high
frequency shrill that fluttered
from his mouth, dull thud from the brim
of a broached squeal. Because child. Because

scared. Because tired. The boy was done
with being shadow, dust film on boot
lip—wanted to be luminous. Sometimes a life
splinters to break. To scatter.
To be.

❧

I see my nephew pressed to the edge
of boyhood, though he looks a man
in my imagination with his flinch
& blush muted, he is still
carved raw from the giggle that over-
takes his toddler body. Thomas
the Tank Engine is this moment's alibi
for letting go. As I watch him now,
I see him still in that faded-cobalt,
whale-imprinted bib he kept soaked
through, but, also, I see the son
I have now, knowing there is no plan.
      The nights   accrue
like gravestones in a tiny plot of land, like light-
less hallways that encircle the Earth, an end-
less tether that yokes the crisp dusk from each
day as it is drained of light: what can never
be seen cast against what can never be
unseen. The promises made against
that other unspoken promise, grief,
made invisible beneath the shadow
of something too large to see—how all
our children share the same erased
name because of it. What leaves them
riddled with everything they cannot see:
piercing   &   rigid   &   always more

weight than anyone predicts. The child
still in the street. It is two minutes & a few
seconds past noon on Canfield Drive
in Ferguson, Missouri, & he is still
right there, in the middle
of the street. Not my nephew. Not my
son.

THERE WERE TWO UNANSWERED
VOICE MAILS FROM YOU

as a white sparrow, trapped inside the heated chamber
of Terminal 3 in O'Hare, zipped past ceiling vents no one
usually sees, while I furiously tried to rebook a flight to nowhere.
Months had slipped by since I last saw you, yet there you were:
wind-chapped grin rising from your favorite chartreuse turtleneck,
early-love smitten, seemingly midjoke, staring down at
something just out of view. I needed to know what you saw.
Sometimes I convince myself I called you back, left
a long message that got cut off, that I stopped by your
door with artichoke hummus. When I first found out
you had AIDS, I prepared for what I would do
when you left. Then, you didn't. It seemed like a gag
we were all in on. An endless joke: death.
But survival is a chameleon—that softly
says *Carpe Noctem* while the knives are still coated
with fresh lime just a short reach from the old, beat-up tub.
I never understood just how carefully your shadow stalked you
each and every second you somehow found a way to live.

FATHER

I

In the basement of the crack house   I used to visit
as an outreach worker   on 121st street in Harlem,
I was convinced   He   refused
to travel north of 96th.   I wrote a letter
to Joanna on her mission   in Taiwan, detailed
each irrefutable   piece of evidence   proving
we are all,   in fact,   alone.
Told her about   the nine-year-old orphan
forced   to sell   her body
for three years   before ending up   just off
Times Square,   discarded   in a dumpster.
I told her about   the eldest son
who answered   a burglar's call   and was shot,
paralyzed   from the waist down.   I asked her
about drought   and famine   and endless
civil wars—what lessons   does His book
refuse?

II

When her heart rate   dropped by half   in less
than a minute,   the population   of our cramped
hospital room   tripling   in a handful of seconds,
I grasped for   anything   that would keep me
upright.   At first,   the wall: cool and steady,
demanding my body   ascend beyond   what seemed
possible.   Then,   nothing,
no one.   I stood   in the waiting room
to the O.R.   waiting   to be called in,
to find out if   my child   had survived.
I spent each second   trying to pull tiny shoe coverings

over my too-large feet.   I confessed   every wrong
of my life   to an empty, overlit room   of steel
and sterile instruments   that all   reflected back
distorted   versions of myself.   I fumbled
for any prayer   I could remember, hoping
that I had all along been   mistaken   about the hollow
blackness   of the infinite sky.   I never wanted
so badly   to have been wrong
about anything   in my life—

       and then   a   disembodied
     voice   called out,   seemingly only to me—
    a tiny growl   at first   that blossomed
    into a wail dwarfing   any thought   my mind
      could   possibly   hold,   any faith
     I'd ever been   so foolish   to claim.

PRAISE

Because my grandmother's
final days lasted twenty-three
years & so we'd rush
each time, say goodbye &
goodbye: *Te quiero*
mucho, Abuelita. Te
adoro. Because my
mother's truest mother
is grief, who taught
her the slack-jawed
abandon of joy. Because
my daughter strung
together a four-syllable
word this afternoon.
Because I say *I love you*
so much to my wife
midfight, & we chuckle
sometimes between
barbs, like we forgot
which characters we
were supposed to play.
Because I was given
a best friend for all of
six years, & we
handwrote letters
each week in bright
ink, dreamed of whose
hair would give way
first. Because the dusk
gave me a reprieve
from the storm on the way

home from daycare today.
Because the rain is a stubborn
guard when I'm most tired &
Grace refuses the chariot
also known as the rickety
stroller that has somehow
not yet quit. Because
Brent metamorphoses
those ticking minutes
everyone else loses
sleep over: shows up
an hour early or makes
me wait while I reread
the menu I've had memorized
for a decade. Because we pretend
we don't know what we'll order, ask
each other, then get the chicken
Pad Thai every damn time. Because
my sister & brother were once
small enough to make a home
of my curled arm, because I loathed
their arrival until that moment
on the seventh floor of Mount
Sinai. Because there are no
half siblings. Because my body
begins to fail a little more each
morning in minute & quiet
increments like gradual,
gorgeous rust. Because
only survival gifts us those
letdowns that remind
a persistent marvel it is
still here. Because I courted
death too long but now

dream of my retirement
porch. Because my son's
scalp at seventy-six seconds
old; the three weeks he barely
slept for more than fifteen
minutes; the lunges that shaped
my quads & calmed his
sobbing just long enough.
Because I have wanted
to be a father as long
as I have feared its weight.
Because I exhale knowing
I cannot fail what I cannot
leave. Because no one
I know has grown more
in three decades than
my father. Because right
now: the oven is performing
its miracles, spring is teasing
us with its slow-building
warmth, my daughter
is coloring in vibrant looping
scrawls that look like cartoon
fireworks or the curls
wreathing the large
eyes she's borrowed
from her mother
& finally:
I am home.

MORNING, RIKERS ISLAND

Physics and light
pierce the hollow stench
of the forgotten gymnasium
stripped naked of clocks.

All the adolescent boys
stop—offer their grief
to each other like water,
glancing out the only window
they all share. A single ray
unfolds its warmth
across the dusty belly
of the thudded parquet,
and here's the miracle:
the sun frees everyone
to sing.

NOTES

"Poem about Death Ending with Reincarnation" only found its way, after countless drafts and many years of false starts, with inspiration from two brilliant poems: Matthew Olzmann's "Mountain Dew Commercial Disguised as a Love Poem" and Tarfia Faizullah's "Poem Full of Worry Ending with My Birth."

"Edge of the Dance Floor" was inspired by the theme of Terrance Hayes's "At Pegasus."

"Abecedarian for the Pimp I Almost Took a Bullet For" was inspired by the form of Natalie Diaz's "Abecedarian Requiring Further Examination of Anglikan Seraphym Subjugation of a Wild Indian Rezervation."

"Thieves in the Temple" was inspired by the theme of Jon Sands's "Highway 71."

"A Blessing for the Internet Troll" quotes hate mail I received through social media, the opening image describing an actual meme that someone posted to my public Facebook page.

"*Mein Kampf* has better reviews than *One Hundred Years of Solitude*" was inspired by a conversation regarding the flawed dimensions of uncurated critical feedback. At the time (in 2012), *Mein Kampf* had a higher average for its starred reviews than *One Hundred Years of Solitude* on Amazon.com. Last I checked, the latter book held a slight edge.

"*Race was not a factor*" quotes excerpts from the testimony of Ferguson, Missouri, police officer Darren Wilson, who killed Michael Brown Jr. on August 9, 2014.

"There Were Two Unanswered Voice Mails from You" is for C. N. S., with all my heart.

"Morning, Rikers Island" is dedicated to the sixteen- and seventeen-year-old boys who were housed in the Robert N. Davoren Complex while incarcerated at Rikers Island and with whom I did writing workshops through Voices Unbroken.

ACKNOWLEDGMENTS

Grateful acknowledgment is made to the editors of the following publications in which these poems, sometimes in earlier versions, first appeared or are forthcoming:

The Acentos Review: "Changing My Name," "When Two Words Fracture the Mirror," "at the playground, on the bus, everywhere"

Atlanta Review: "Underground"

Backbone Press: "Hijito"

The Big Windows Review: "Poem about Death Ending with Reincarnation"

BuzzFeed Reader: "What Happened"

CHORUS: A Literary Mixtape: "Hand-Stitch"

Crab Creek Review: "Pronounced"

Cultural Weekly: "C(h)ord"

Glass: A Journal of Poetry: "Above the Speed Limit"

The Journal: "Elegy for the Longest Year," "Revisionist," "Inertia"

Levee Magazine: "Eighteen Images around the Text Message to Your Mother"

Menacing Hedge: "After the cab driver asks me—*How you like Black pussy?*"

New England Review: "Last Sundays at Bootleggers"

North American Review: "There Were Two Unanswered Voice Mails from You"

The Ocotillo Review: "Edge of the Dance Floor"

Painted Bride Quarterly: "Black Hair," "Interracial in Flatbush, Brooklyn," "Morning, Rikers Island"

Paterson Literary Review: "The Afternoon You Moved Out"

Philadelphia Stories: "Murambi," "*Race was not a factor*"

Prism Review: "Thieves in the Temple," "A Blessing for the Internet Troll," "Praise"

Psaltery & Lyre: "Father"

Radius: "Cool"

The Rumpus: "When Our Black Son Arrives"

Smartish Pace: "Kigali Memorial," "*Mein Kampf* has better reviews than *One Hundred Years of Solitude*"

Solstice Literary Magazine: "Before the Last Shot"

Southword Journal: "Abecedarian for the Pimp I Almost Took a Bullet For"

The Yale Review: "Native Tongue"

Some of the above poems appeared in the chapbook *Hijito* (Platypus Press, 2019).

"Pronounced" was reprinted in *Ink Knows No Borders: Poems of the Immigrant and Refugee Experience* (Seven Stories Press, 2019).

"Hijito" and "Before the Last Shot" were reprinted in *The BreakBeat Poets Vol. 4: LatiNext* (Haymarket Books, 2020).

This book could never have existed without an abundance of generosity, support, challenges, belief, and, above all, unconditional love from a vibrant universe of people I will forever hold dear—

My graduate school mentors in the MFA Program for Writers at Warren Wilson College, especially: C. Dale Young, Rodney Jones, Gabrielle Calvocoressi, Sandra Lim, Roger Reeves, Alan Shapiro, Matthew Olzmann, Martha Rhodes, Debra Allbery, and, of course, Ellen Bryant Voigt.

Natasha Trethewey: I've been awed by your work since first reading *Native Guard* so many years ago. I never could have dreamed that your thoughtful editorial eye would bring my full-length debut to the world. I am infinitely grateful.

The stunning team at the University of Wisconsin Press: Dennis Lloyd, Ivan Babanovski, Kaitlin Svabek, Ron Wallace, Sean Bishop, Adam Mehring, Jennifer Conn, Sheila McMahon, and so many others behind the scenes. I am so humbled and overwhelmed with gratitude that this book found a home with UWP.

My heroes-beloveds, who teach/remind me, each day, not just how to write but how to live: Angel Nafis, Adam Falkner, Caroline Rothstein, Mahogany L. Browne, Jive Poetic, Felice Belle, Jeanann Verlee, Syreeta McFadden, Ellison "Black Cracker" Glenn, Shira Erlichman, Jon Sands, Rico Frederick, Eboni Hogan, Jamaal St. John, Sarah Kay, Andrea Gibson, Geoff Kagan Trenchard, Elizabeth Acevedo, Bassey Ikpi, Katie Kramer, Melissa Pavri, Cortney Lamar Charleston, José Olivarez, Hieu Minh Nguyen, Lauren Whitehead, Carvens Lissaint, Lemon Andersen, Phil Kaye, Reed Swier, Paul Tran, Denice Frohman, Emily Kagan Trenchard, Aracelis Girmay, Patrick Rosal, Lynne Procope, Sofía Snow, Warren Longmire, Dr. Alysia Harris, Aysha El-Shamayleh, Dr. Joshua Bennett, Justin Reilly, Benjamin

Alisuag, Lindsey Rosin Passman, Victoria Ford, Rob Yang, Tahani Salah, Lily Chiu-Watson, Leigh Lucas, Mike Goetzman, Amy Lin, Idrissa Simmonds, Shannon K. Winston, Sonya Larsen, Perry Janes, Cynthia Dewi Oka, Jasminne Mendez, Sevé Torres, Arhm Choi Wild, Samantha Thornhill, Aziza Barnes, Aaron Samuels, Jayson Smith, Mikal Lee, Cristin O'Keefe Aptowicz, Karen Jaime, Nile St. John, Julian Curry, Maggie Ambrosino-Sands, Rich Villar, Elana Bell, Jai Chakrabarti, Jamaal May, Andrew Kramer, Marty McConnell, t'ai freedom ford, Abena Koomson, Fish Vargas, April Ranger, C. Bain, Ove Salcedo, Obinna Obilo, Joy Dyer, Tracey Gilbert, Ibraheem Basir, Sabrina Austin-Edouard, Pablo Sierra, Mohamed Sow, Dr. Stephen Danley, Ivy Sole, Justin Ching, Ilana Millner, Sruthi Sadhujan, Tiffany Kang, Darian Dauchan, Tara Hardy, Afra Atiq, Alixa García, Safia Elhillo, Kamilah Aisha Moon, Anthony Morales, Kelly Tsai, Noel Quiñones, Regie Cabico, Javon Johnson, G. Yamazawa, April Jones, George Watsky, Sekou Andrews, Tara Betts, Mike McGee, Shihan Van Clief, Erik "Zork" Alan, Anacaona, Vanessa Hidary, Beau Sia, Chinaka Hodge, Ken Arkind, Anis Mojgani, Rachel Eliza Griffiths, Dwayne Morgan, Joanna Hoffman, Kahlil Almustafa, Tshaka Campbell, Pages Matam, Nate Marshall, Tina Chang, Danez Smith, Tyehimba Jess, Mayda Del Valle, Walidah Imarisha, Don Leake, Clint Smith, Mak Manaka, Luka Lesson, Raymond Antrobus, Ocean Vuong, Charlotte Hill O'Neal, and, of course, Rachel McKibbens.

Martín Espada: my poetic life is ever indebted to your transcendent example, far beyond that high school assembly where you saw me and gave me permission/the push to be a writer.

Patricia Smith: I've never witnessed a more luminous or generous literary citizen, role model, and mentor.

Saul Williams and Sonja Sohn: your work in *Slam* ignited the poet I didn't know I was.

Eduardo C. Corral: You were the first to open a door for this manuscript and get it out to the world. I continue to be astonished by your work and your spirit.

Tamilla Woodard: I've never encountered anyone more generous or brilliant.

Melody Guy: you've taught me so much about writing and kindness.

Rene Alegria: thank you for being such a fierce champion of my vision and my work.

Travers Johnson: thank you for fighting for my memoir and gifting me this belief in myself.

Spike Lee: inspired always by your loyalty and your guts.

My longtime and loyal supporters—who've been packing my solo shows in New York City since the early 2000s, sharing my videos and published poems, tattooing lines from pieces I've forgotten I wrote, and who are holding a signed copy of this book in their hands—I am only able to continue this artist's life because of your unyielding support. I am so grateful for and humbled by your belief in me and what I do.

Tireless champions of my work, who've made this full-time creative life possible for fifteen years and counting: Sue Boxrud (the G.O.A.T.), Scott Bass, Chris Schuler, Christina Bravo, and the entire Bass/Schuler Entertainment team; Adam Bricault, Joshua Barnes, Victoria Kwan, Victor Arias, Luis Galilei, and the rest of the Dream Team at Edelman; Kate Berner, Liz Fithian, Alysyn Reinhardt, and everyone at the Penguin Random House Speakers Bureau; Bill Shinker, Megan Newman, Lisa Johnson, Megan Halpern, Jessica Chun, Alan Walker, and everyone at Gotham Books (back in the day!) and the brilliant folks at Penguin Random House; my 40 Acres and a Mule family; and, last but not least, Michelle Tudor, Peter Barnfather, and Platypus Press.

My Excelano Project (EP!) family at the University of Pennsylvania and across the world.

My dearest friends who've loved me and held me up for decades, especially on those hardest of days: Brent, Leila, Jojo, Eric, Arnett, Kenda, Jess, Iso, and so many more. You know who you are.

Dearest ones, who make me want to be better every day: Mafaz Al-Suwaidan, Dr. Jasmin Zine, Yusuf Zine, Asma Bala, and Jeff Perera.

Framily: Shameeka, Becca, Cat, Angela, Charla, Toren, Corina, B. G., Benny and Malan, Damion, and the list goes on . . .

My beloved familia in Florida, Colombia, and beyond—I can't imagine this life without your ceaseless laughter, support, and love. I am so proud to be tu primo, tu sobrino.

My cherished family: Moms, Pops, Jaime, Maurice, Carter, Hunter, Naye, Marcell, Court, Will, Leslie, Bill, and Thomas—never in-laws, forever my in-loves.

Mommy, Papi, Sarita, Karin, Nico, and Mayita: your love and belief in me has saved me more times than you will ever know. You inspire me to be a better father, son, brother, and human being. There is nothing I could ever write that would express what I feel for each of you.

And, finally, my everythings: Whitney, Grace, and Gabriel. I am not possible without you.

Everything I am and aspire to become is for you.

My heart is yours, always.

Wisconsin Poetry Series
Edited by Ronald Wallace and Sean Bishop

How the End First Showed (B) • D. M. Aderibigbe

New Jersey (B) • Betsy Andrews

Salt (B) • Renée Ashley

Horizon Note (B) • Robin Behn

About Crows (FP) • Craig Blais

Mrs. Dumpty (FP) • Chana Bloch

The Declarable Future (4L) • Jennifer Boyden

The Mouths of Grazing Things (B) • Jennifer Boyden

Help Is on the Way (4L) • John Brehm

No Day at the Beach • John Brehm

Sea of Faith (B) • John Brehm

Reunion (FP) • Fleda Brown

Brief Landing on the Earth's Surface (B) • Juanita Brunk

Ejo: Poems, Rwanda, 1991–1994 (FP) • Derick Burleson

Jagged with Love (B) • Susanna Childress

Almost Nothing to Be Scared Of (4L) • David Clewell

The Low End of Higher Things • David Clewell

Now We're Getting Somewhere (FP) • David Clewell

Taken Somehow by Surprise (4L) • David Clewell

Borrowed Dress (FP) • Cathy Colman

Dear Terror, Dear Splendor • Melissa Crowe

Places/Everyone (B) • Jim Daniels

Show and Tell • Jim Daniels

Darkroom (B) • Jazzy Danziger

And Her Soul Out of Nothing (B) • Olena Kalytiak Davis

My Favorite Tyrants (B) • Joanne Diaz

Talking to Strangers (B) • Patricia Dobler

(B) = Winner of the Brittingham Prize in Poetry

(FP) = Winner of the Felix Pollak Prize in Poetry

(4L) = Winner of the Four Lakes Prize in Poetry

The Golden Coin (4L) • Alan Feldman

Immortality (4L) • Alan Feldman

A Sail to Great Island (FP) • Alan Feldman

The Word We Used for It (B) • Max Garland

A Field Guide to the Heavens (B) • Frank X. Gaspar

The Royal Baker's Daughter (FP) • Barbara Goldberg

Fractures (FP) • Carlos Andrés Gómez

Gloss • Rebecca Hazelton

Funny (FP) • Jennifer Michael Hecht

Queen in Blue • Ambalila Hemsell

The Legend of Light (FP) • Bob Hicok

Sweet Ruin (B) • Tony Hoagland

Partially Excited States (FP) • Charles Hood

Ripe (FP) • Roy Jacobstein

Perigee (B) • Diane Kerr

Saving the Young Men of Vienna (B) • David Kirby

Ganbatte (FP) • Sarah Kortemeier

Falling Brick Kills Local Man (FP) • Mark Kraushaar

Last Seen (FP) • Jacqueline Jones LaMon

The Lightning That Strikes the Neighbors' House (FP) • Nick Lantz

You, Beast (B) • Nick Lantz

The Explosive Expert's Wife • Shara Lessley

The Unbeliever (B) • Lisa Lewis

Slow Joy (B) • Stephanie Marlis

Acts of Contortion (B) • Anna George Meek

Bardo (B) • Suzanne Paola

Meditations on Rising and Falling (B) • Philip Pardi

Old and New Testaments (B) • Lynn Powell

Season of the Second Thought (FP) • Lynn Powell

A Path between Houses (B) • Greg Rappleye

The Book of Hulga (FP) • Rita Mae Reese

Why Can't It Be Tenderness (FP) • Michelle Brittan Rosado

Don't Explain (FP) • Betsy Sholl

House of Sparrows: New and Selected Poems (4L) • Betsy Sholl

Late Psalm • Betsy Sholl

Otherwise Unseeable (4L) • Betsy Sholl

Blood Work (FP) • Matthew Siegel

Fruit (4L) • Bruce Snider

The Year We Studied Women (FP) • Bruce Snider

Bird Skin Coat (B) • Angela Sorby

The Sleeve Waves (FP) • Angela Sorby

If the House (B) • Molly Spencer

Wait (B) • Alison Stine

Hive (B) • Christina Stoddard

The Red Virgin: A Poem of Simone Weil (B) • Stephanie Strickland

The Room Where I Was Born (B) • Brian Teare

Fragments in Us: Recent and Earlier Poems (FP) • Dennis Trudell

The Apollonia Poems (4L) • Judith Vollmer

Level Green (B) • Judith Vollmer

Reactor • Judith Vollmer

Voodoo Inverso (FP) • Mark Wagenaar

Hot Popsicles • Charles Harper Webb

Liver (FP) • Charles Harper Webb

The Blue Hour (B) • Jennifer Whitaker

Centaur (B) • Greg Wrenn

Pocket Sundial (B) • Lisa Zeidner

Carlos Andrés Gómez is a Colombian American poet from New York City. He is the author of the chapbook *Hijito* (2019), selected by Eduardo C. Corral as the winner of the 2018 Broken River Prize; and the memoir *Man Up: Reimagining Modern Manhood* (2012). His honors and awards include the Sandy Crimmins National Prize for Poetry, the Fischer National Poetry Prize, the Lucille Clifton Poetry Prize, and the *Atlanta Review* International Poetry Prize, as well as fellowships from the Andrew W. Mellon Foundation, Voices of Our Nation Arts Foundation, and the Jerome Foundation. Gómez has been published in *New England Review, Beloit Poetry Journal, Yale Review, BuzzFeed Reader, CHORUS: A Literary Mixtape* (2012), and elsewhere. He is a graduate of the University of Pennsylvania and the MFA Program for Writers at Warren Wilson College.

For more, please visit **CarlosLive.com**.

Connect with Carlos on Twitter & Instagram: **@CarlosAGLive**